ALPHABATTY

Riddles from A to Z

by Rick and Ann Walton
pictures by Susan Slattery Burke

Lerner Publications Company · Minneapolis

To STEPHEN, a grade A kid because HE SPENT the time   —R.W. & A.W.

*To my wonderful daughter, Shea, for her incredible inspiration
in this first year of her life*   —S.S.B.

This book is available in two editions:
Library binding by Lerner Publications Company
Soft cover by First Avenue Editions
241 First Avenue North
Minneapolis, MN 55401

Library of Congress Cataloging-in-Publication Data

Walton, Rick.
  Alphabatty : riddles from A to Z / by Rick & Ann Walton ; pictures by Susan
Slattery Burke.

    p.   cm.
  Summary: Presents riddles about letters of the alphabet, such as "What
letter will give you a lift? The L-evator."
  ISBN 0-8225-2335-3 (lib. bdg.)
  ISBN 0-8225-9593-1 (pbk.)
  1. Riddles, Juvenile. 2. Alphabet—Humor. [1. Alphabet—Wit and humor.
2. Riddles.] I. Walton, Ann, 1963-   . II. Burke, Susan Slattery, III. III. Title.
PN6371.5W345   1991
818'.5402—dc20
                                                90-28791
                                                  CIP

Manufactured in the United States of America
                                                    AC

1 2 3 4 5 6 7 8 9 10 00 99 98 97 96 95 94 93 92 91

Q: Why is it easy to see
the letter E?

A: Because it's at the end
of your NOSE.

Q: What do you get if you're allergic to the letter B?
A: B-hives.

Q: What's the best way to shoot an L-shaped arrow?
A: With an L-bow.

Q: What two letters are all right?
A: O K.

Q: Why do O and M like each other?

A: Because they have so much in COMMON.

Q: How should you feel if a letter N gives you a pat on the back?

A: N-couraged.

Q: How do you feel if a giant letter D sits on you?

A: D-pressed.

Q: What did the letter T say to the pencil?
A: "You've crossed me for the last time!"

Q: Why is the letter A at the head of the alphabet?
A: Because it's in CHARGE.

Q: Why are there so few letter Q's in the dictionary?
A: Because Q is not in DEMAND.

Q: What letter is difficult to figure out?
A: Mister-E.

Q: What do you get when you cross the letter M with the king of cats?

A: The M-purrer.

Q: What is the capital of France?

A: The letter F.

Q: When did the American patriots celebrate a letter?

A: At the Boston T Party.

Q: Why were there only twenty-four letters in the alphabet 200 years ago?

A: Because U and I weren't there.

Q: How do we know Hamlet had trouble spelling rabbit?

A: Because he asked himself, "Two B's or not two B's."

MLE: "How did you feel when you got a D on your test?

KT: D-graded!

IV: "How did you feel when you stuck the D in the lamp?

DD: "D-lighted!"

Q: How would you feel if you ate a lot of P's?

A: P's full.

Q: Why does the letter Z frequently get lost?

A: Because it's always in a HAZE.

Q: What do you find twice as much of in nighttime as in daytime?

A: The letter T.

Q: What can you always find in the middle of the night?

A: The letter G.

COOKIES

Q: What should you feed the letter C?
A: C-food.

Q: Why will the letter A send food into space?
A: Because it will make your lunch LAUNCH.

Q: Why should you never eat a treat that has the letter H on it?
A: Because it makes the treat a THREAT.

Q: Why is an E a welcome sight to a hungry person?
A: Because it turns a fast into a FEAST.

Q: What letter is always in hot water?
A: T.

Q: What do beginning gamblers have to learn?
A: Their alpha-bet.

Q: Why don't spies like the letter S?
A: Because it makes their lip SLIP.

Q: Why should you never put an S on a lime?
A: Because it makes the lime SLIME.

Q: What letters of the alphabet should you stay away from?

A: N M E.

Q: Why should you give the letter R to a fiend?

A: Because it will make the fiend a FRIEND.

Q: Why do uncles and aunts like to take the letter E away from a naughty niece?

A: Because they know that it will make their niece NICE.

Q: What do you get if someone hits you with a letter I?

A: An I-sore.

Q: What letter reminds you of looking in the mirror?

A: W.

Q: Why are the letters T and E so popular?

A: Because they're always in STYLE and never out of DATE.

Q: Why are L and I so straight?

A: Because everyone keeps them in LINE.

Q: What happens when Ben gets hit by a letter T?

A: Ben becomes BENT.

Q: Why does Nat's mother like the letter E?

A: Because it makes Nat NEAT.

Q: Why should you take an R away from Fred if he's hungry?

A: Because it gets Fred FED.

Q: Why is the letter S easy to recognize?

A: Because it appears everywhere in PERSON.

Q: Why should you throw an S at a cat if you want it to go away?

A: Because it will make the cat SCAT.

Q: How do you feel if the letter N puts a curse on you?

A: N-chanted.

Q: Which letter is magical?

A: The Fair-E.

Q: Why are the letters L and O so close?

A: Because they're in LOVE.

Q: Why will the letter C never go straight?

A: Because it goes in CIRCLES.

Q: Why should a kid never carry the letter S while he's walking on ice?

A: Because it'll make the kid SKID.

Q: Why can the letter T run forever?

A: Because it's always in CONDITION and never out of BREATH.

Q: Why should you never get in a plane with a letter T?

A: Because it will turn the plane into a PLANET.

Q: Why should you always carry a W with you if you're in a hurry?

A: Because it will make your heels WHEELS.

Q: What are there four of in every engine but never found in any car?

A: The letter E.

Q: If you want to see a lot of letter D's, what should you do?

A: Take a D-tour.

Q: What letter will give you a lift?
A: The L-evator.

Q: Why is an extra A a nice thing for someone to have?
A: It turns any place into a PALACE.

Q: What letters live in Tokyo?
A: Japan E's.

Q: Why doesn't the letter H get any visitors?
A: Because it's in the middle of NOWHERE.

Q: What letter is a game for birds?
A: Crow-K.

Q: What letter likes to swing?
A: The chimpan-Z.

Q: What letter roamed the
plains years ago?
A: The Buffal-O.

Q: What's the best way to shine the letter B?

A: With B's-wax.

Q: What three letters do athletes like?

A: N R G.

Q: What letters perform in the circus?

A: The trap-E's.

Q: What do you get if you plant a letter C?

A: C-weed.

Q: Why are the letters B and D like a beach?

A: Because they're found next to the C.

Q: What should you do if you accidentally drop your letter C down a well?

A: Go deep-C fishing.

Q: What do beginning fishers have to learn?

A: Their alpha-bait.

Q: If you're sailing in the ocean, why is it better to have a T than a life preserver?

A: Because if you fall into the ocean, you can take out your T and turn the sea into a SEAT, then you can just sit and wait for someone to come rescue you.

Q: Why is the letter V never late?
A: Because it always shows up in ADVANCE.

Q: Where does the letter C go swimming?
A: At the C-shore.

Q: What happened when the J suddenly came onto the baseball field?
A: It made the ump JUMP.

Q: What will we see at the end of time?
A: The letter E.

Q: Why is the letter L healthy?
A: Because all's well that ends WELL.

ABOUT THE AUTHORS

Rick and Ann Walton love to read, travel, play guitar, study foreign languages, and write for children. Rick also collects books and writes music while Ann knits and does origami. They live in Provo, Utah, where Ann is a computer programmer and Rick is erasing all the A's from the encyclopedia. They have two unbelievable children.

A K S R Y F

ABOUT THE ARTIST

Susan Slattery Burke loves to illustrate fun-loving characters, especially animals. To her, each of them has a personality all its own. Her satisfaction comes when the characters come to life for the reader as well. Susan lives in Minneapolis, Minnesota, with her husband, their daughter, and their dog and cat. A graduate of the University of Minnesota, Susan enjoys sculpting, travel, illustrating, chasing her daughter, and being outdoors.

C L Q Z E W

If you like **Alphabatty.** you'll love
these other **You Must Be Joking** riddle books:

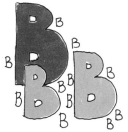

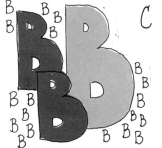